Sensation!

See, hear, touch, taste, smell

Nepeti Nicanor

J·A·W·S
DISCOVERY

Heinemann Educational Publishers
Halley Court, Jordan Hill, Oxford OX2 8EJ
A part of Harcourt Education Limited

OXFORD MELBOURNE AUCKLAND
JOHANNESBURG GABARONE KUALA LUMPUR
PORTSMOUTH (NH) USA CHICAGO

Series Editor: Karen Morrison
Cover photographs by Science Photo Library and Peter Hassall (girl)
The background photograph shows a magnified view of rod and cone cells
in the retina of the human eye.

Design by Jackie Hill @ 320 Design

Illustrations by Ian Lusted

Photographs courtesy of Peter Hassall (pages 4/5); Science Photo Library
(page 10); Illustrative Options (pages 12, 19, 20/21, 24/25); Gallo Images
(page 14); BBC Natural History Picture Library (page 26 – Kirk's dik dik and
pages 26/27 cheetahs); Oxford Scientific Films (page 27 – snake, page 28);
NHPA (page 30 – large picture); FLPA (page 30 – two small pictures).

Printed and bound in the UK by Ashford Colour Press Limited.

ISBN 0 435 89852 3
04 05 06 07 8 7 6 5 4 3

About the author

Nepeti Nicanor lives with her daughter, Leila, in a house in Windhoek in
which every room is painted a different colour. Nepeti has lived,
worked and studied in Namibia, England and Zimbabwe. She
trained as a bio-chemist and has taught science in schools. Nepeti
also works as a writer, a publisher, and a human rights activist.

Contents

Our five senses

Can you see, smell, taste, hear and touch? These are your five senses and you will find out more about them in this book.

The people in the picture are using their senses: seeing, smelling, tasting, hearing and touching.

◎ Seeing – they are watching the drummer.

◎ Tasting and smelling – the boy is eating an ice-cream.

◎ Hearing – they are listening to the music.

◎ Touching and feeling – the drummer is playing with his hands.

Our senses help us to avoid danger, listen to sounds, eat, read and enjoy ourselves! Our senses also let us feel pain. We know if something we touch is hot or cold, wet or dry, smooth or rough.

Just imagine...

Imagine that you lost one of your five senses. Which sense would you miss most?

5

The brain

We use different parts of the body for each sense. The sense organs are the eyes, ears, nose, tongue and the skin. The brain controls the sense organs. When these organs sense things, messages are sent along the nerves to the brain. The brain allows us to understand the messages and feel the sensations. For example, when we touch something hot, our brain tells us to move our hand away quickly. A dog barks when it hears someone coming.

When our brain receives messages from our sense organs, it tells us what response to make. For example, when we see a red traffic light, we know the car has to stop. But sometimes it is difficult for our brains to understand the message it receives. Look at the picture below. This is called an 'optical illusion' because your eyes give a false message to your brain.

Hearing cent

Smell centre

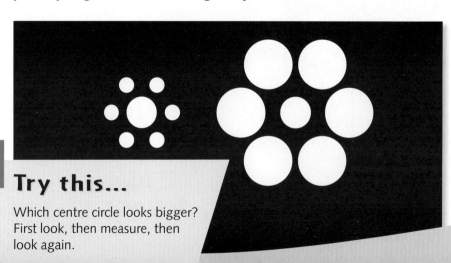

Try this...

Which centre circle looks bigger? First look, then measure, then look again.

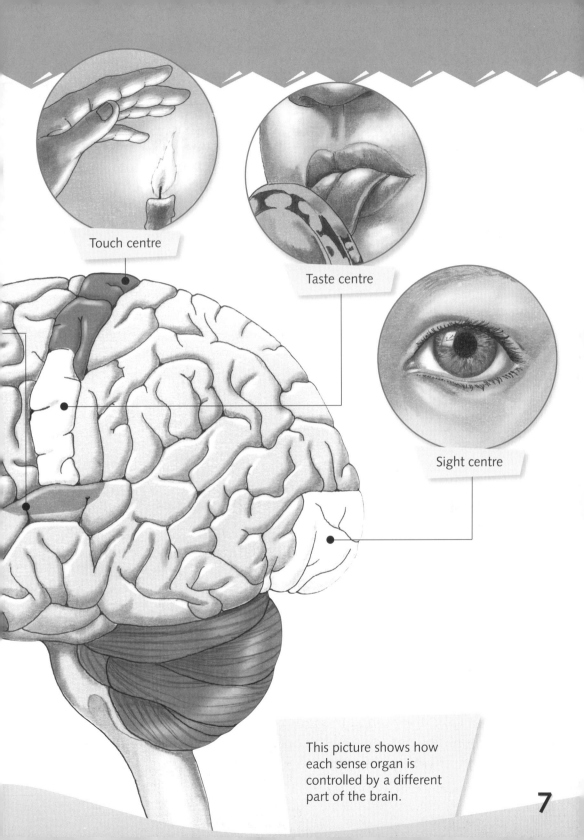

Touch centre

Taste centre

Sight centre

This picture shows how each sense organ is controlled by a different part of the brain.

7

Have you ever thought about how you use your eyes? They allow you to recognise shapes and colours, to see things that are close by or far away and also to tell whether things are moving or still. Your eyes also help you to recognise people and to recognise danger.

1 Rays of light enter the eye through the pupil

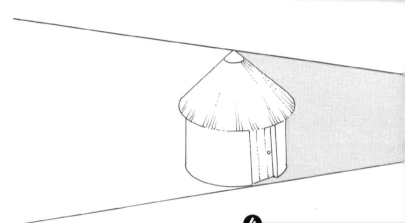

4 The optic nerve then sends the message to the brain

How do our eyes work?

The eye needs light to see. When you look at things, rays of light enter your eye through the pupil. The pupil is a hole that looks like a black circle in the middle of the eye. The light then passes through a lens which is shaped like a see-through pill with curved sides. The curved lens bends the rays of light to form an upside-down image on the retina. The retina is a layer of seeing cells at the back of the eye.

5 The brain turns the picture the correct way up again

When the seeing cells in the retina receive the bent light, they send messages to the brain through the nerve called the optic nerve. The brain then turns the picture the correct way up again.

This picture shows how we see.

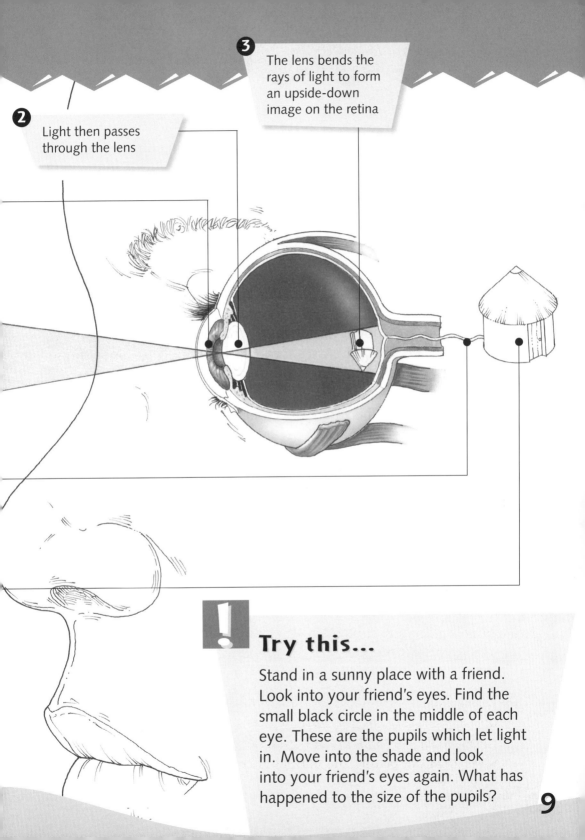

3 The lens bends the rays of light to form an upside-down image on the retina

2 Light then passes through the lens

Try this...

Stand in a sunny place with a friend. Look into your friend's eyes. Find the small black circle in the middle of each eye. These are the pupils which let light in. Move into the shade and look into your friend's eyes again. What has happened to the size of the pupils?

How do we see colour?

The retina in the eye contains three types of colour-seeing cells. These are shaped like cones. Each type of cone cell is sensitive to either red or blue or green light. We see different colours when the different types of cone cells are sensitised or 'triggered off' at the same time. For example, when both red and green light enters the eyes, we see yellow. The human eye can see about ten million different colour shades.

Perhaps it is difficult to imagine that light is made of different colours. Yet we know that sunlight is made of a mixture of colours. When sunlight passes through raindrops, the raindrops act like tiny lenses which bend and scatter the sunlight into the seven colours of the rainbow: red, orange, yellow, green, blue, indigo and violet. This range of colours is called the light spectrum.

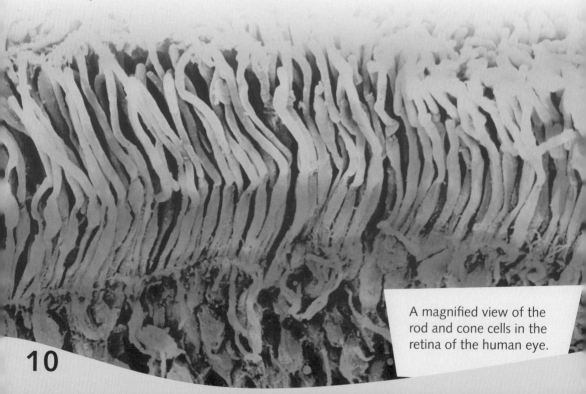

A magnified view of the rod and cone cells in the retina of the human eye.

Seeing in the dark

As well as cone cells, there are also rod cells in the retina. These seeing cells need very little light to work. They help us to see in the dark. Rod cells cannot recognise colour, so things look black, grey or white when we use these cells.

Two eyes are better than one

We see better when we use both our eyes. Our eyes are in different positions so that each eye sees a slightly different picture. When the brain fits the two pictures together, it builds a deeper, three-dimensional (3D) image rather than a flat image. If we only had one eye in the centre of our face, things we see would look much flatter. Because we have two eyes, we are able to judge the position of things we see more accurately.

Chameleons can move their eyes separately and can see in a complete circle around themselves. We cannot see behind ourselves without turning our heads.

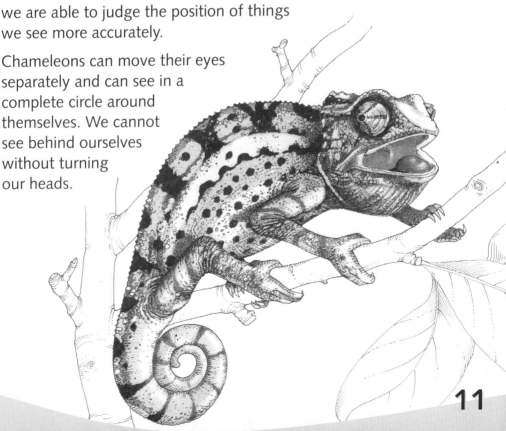

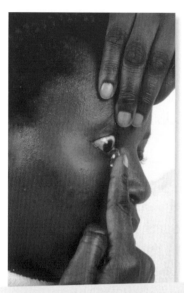

Inserting a contact lens

When someone with normal eyesight looks at something, a clear image forms on the retina at the back of the eye.

However, not everyone can see clearly. Some people are long-sighted and can only clearly see things that are far away. Other people are short-sighted and can only clearly see things that are nearby. When people are long-sighted or short-sighted, the lens part of the eye cannot bend the light to form a sharp, focused image on the retina. These people need glasses or contact lenses to see properly. The lenses in the glasses help to make a sharp image on the retina. Contact lenses are clear plastic discs that rest on the eyeball and act like glasses to correct eyesight.

Colour blindness

People who are colour blind often cannot tell the difference between red and green objects. This is because some people only have two types of cone cells instead of three. This makes it difficult for them to tell the difference between some colours.

Blindness

Some people are born blind and cannot see at all. Others may lose their sight because of accidents or diseases. Blindness is a big problem in some areas of Africa where there are biting blackflies in rivers. When the flies bite people, they leave tiny eggs. If the eggs travel to the eye and hatch there, they cause a disease called River Blindness.

Cataracts

Have you seen old people with a milky-coloured growth in their eyes? These are cataracts. The lens of the eye becomes cloudy and forms a cataract which prevents light from passing through the lens to the retina. This stops the person seeing. Cataracts can be successfully removed by an operation. Some diseases, such as diabetes and rickets, may also cause cataracts.

Night blindness

The rod cells need vitamin A to work properly. People who have a shortage of vitamin A may not be able to see very well at night. This is why eating food with enough vitamin A helps people to see better at night. Foods like carrots, pumpkins, pawpaw, palm oil, spinach, milk and eggs are all rich in vitamin A.

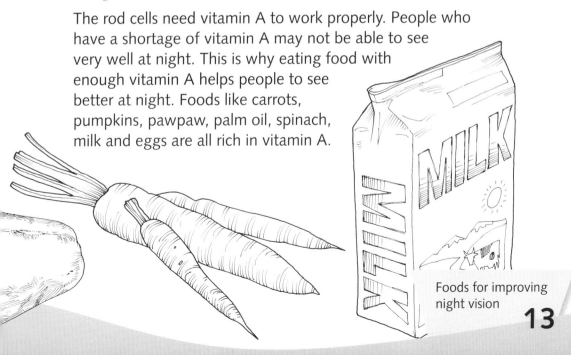

Foods for improving night vision

The nose knows!

People can recognise about 4 000 different smells. Our sense of smell is so powerful it can often tell us what things are before we see them. Think about someone cooking – the smell is often enough to let you know what is being prepared.

Smell is very important because it helps us to recognise things and people. Every person smells differently. A baby can recognise its mother by her smell.

Smell can also protect us from danger. We can smell when food is rotten and the bad smell stops us from eating it. We can smell smoke and burning and that can warn us that there is a fire.

Some people have a very finely developed sense of smell. Trained wine tasters and perfume makers can often recognise up to 10 000 different smells!

How it works

Your nose and brain work together so that you can smell things that are in gas or vapour form. Inside our noses there are olfactory cells. These are special cells covered by wet mucus and little hairs. To smell an onion, for example, the vapours from the onion mix with the air and enter our noses when we breathe. Inside the nose, the onion vapours mix again with the wet mucus around the smell cells. This causes the cells to change and send a message to the brain. The brain then tells us that we are smelling onion.

Every substance causes a different change in the smelling cells so the message to the brain is different each time. Our brains recognise and remember smells that we have smelled before.

Sinus

Olfactory cells

Nerves to brain

Nasal cavity

Nerves for tasting

Tongue

A cut-away picture of the head to show the organs used in smelling

We can recognise different tastes with our tongues. The taste buds on the tongue help us to identify four basic tastes – sweet, salty, bitter and sour. The different taste buds are found around the edges of the tongue, but the centre of the tonguc is not involved in tasting at all. There are also taste buds scattered around the inside of the mouth. For example, the main taste buds for sour and bitter flavours are in the roof of the mouth.

How do we taste?

The tongue's taste buds are little bumps that are linked to the brain by nerves. The taste buds can only recognise tastes when they are in liquid form. So, when we put food into our mouths it is mixed with saliva to form a liquid that we can taste. When the saliva touches the taste buds, the nerves send messages to the brain. The brain tells us what we are tasting.

Bitter taste buds

Sour taste buds

Salty taste buds

Sweet taste buds

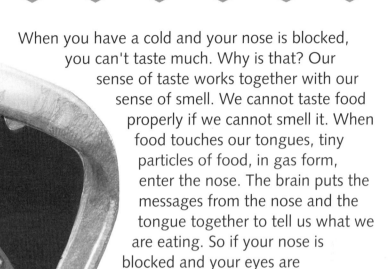

When you have a cold and your nose is blocked, you can't taste much. Why is that? Our sense of taste works together with our sense of smell. We cannot taste food properly if we cannot smell it. When food touches our tongues, tiny particles of food, in gas form, enter the nose. The brain puts the messages from the nose and the tongue together to tell us what we are eating. So if your nose is blocked and your eyes are blindfolded, you will not be able to taste the difference between a slice of raw potato and a piece of apple.

Try this...

Blindfold a friend and ask them to hold their own nose. Give them a taste of: bread, mango, banana, milk, water, tea. Can they tell you what they are tasting?

Different areas of the tongue have different taste buds

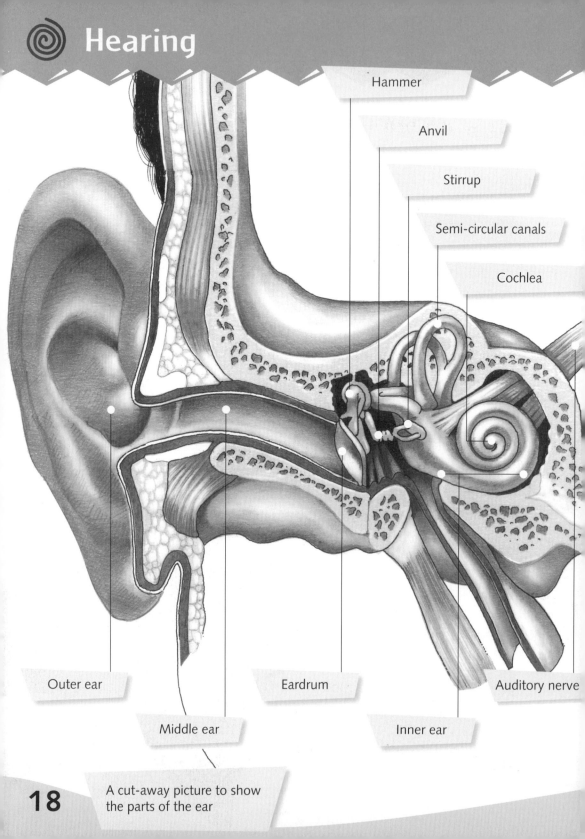

Hammer

Anvil

Stirrup

Semi-circular canals

Cochlea

Outer ear

Eardrum

Auditory nerve

Middle ear

Inner ear

A cut-away picture to show
the parts of the ear

How do we hear?

To understand how people hear, you need to understand how sound moves through air. All sounds are made by vibrations. When we talk, we make vibrations. These vibrations move through the air as sound waves, which travel to people's ears.

Our ear is divided into three parts: the outer, the middle and the inner ear.

The outer ear collects sound waves travelling through the air. The sound waves pass into the ear and cause the eardrum to vibrate. The vibrations are made stronger by three little bones inside the ear: the hammer, the anvil and the stirrup. The stirrup sends the vibrations to the fluid in the inner ear. Vibrations in this fluid are felt by hearing cells inside the cochlea and messages are sent to the brain for interpretation. Try to follow this on the diagram.

Did you know...

Messages need to come from both ears for the brain to be able to tell the direction a sound is coming from.

Try this...

If you hold a shell or a cup to your ear you will hear the sound of the blood flowing around inside your head. This sounds a bit like the sea.

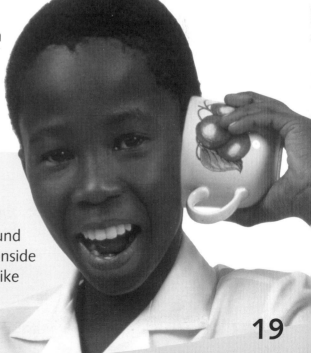

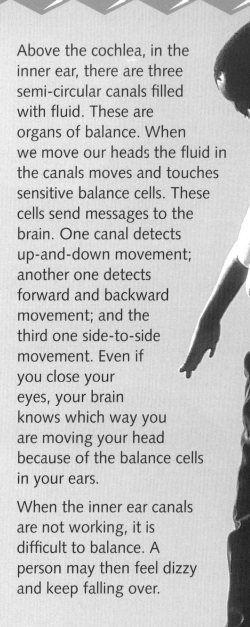

Above the cochlea, in the inner ear, there are three semi-circular canals filled with fluid. These are organs of balance. When we move our heads the fluid in the canals moves and touches sensitive balance cells. These cells send messages to the brain. One canal detects up-and-down movement; another one detects forward and backward movement; and the third one side-to-side movement. Even if you close your eyes, your brain knows which way you are moving your head because of the balance cells in your ears.

When the inner ear canals are not working, it is difficult to balance. A person may then feel dizzy and keep falling over.

Have you heard . . .

The loudness of sound is measured in decibels (dB). The decibel was named after Alexander Graham Bell who invented the telephone. The pictures in the table show you how loud some sounds are. Very loud sounds can damage your ears, and sounds above 120dB can cause pain.

The louder the noise, the higher the decibels (dB)

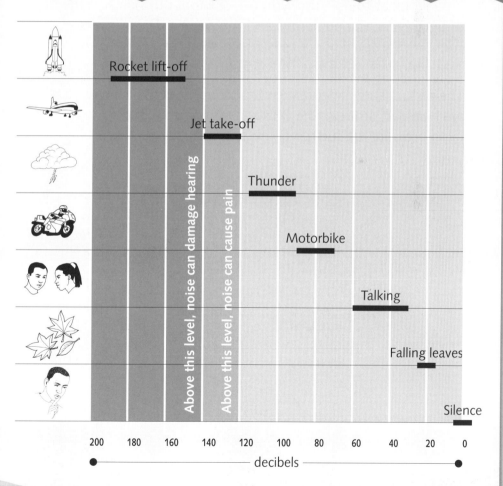

Rocket lift-off

Jet take-off

Thunder

Motorbike

Talking

Falling leaves

Silence

Above this level, noise can damage hearing

Above this level, noise can cause pain

| 200 | 180 | 160 | 140 | 120 | 100 | 80 | 60 | 40 | 20 | 0 |

decibels

The skin

The skin is the organ of touch. Tiny nerve cells in the skin allow us to feel things around us. They allow us to feel cold, heat, pain, rough and smooth things. Our skin also senses if it is being touched lightly or with pressure. Our skin allows us to feel things around us.

How does it work?

If you look at the picture, you can see that our skin is made up of two layers, the epidermis and the dermis. These layers contain very small nerve cells which send messages to the brain. Most of our sense of touch is in the epidermis.

The picture shows nerve cells that sense touch, pain and heat are near the surface. The cells for sensing cold and deep pressure are further below the surface.

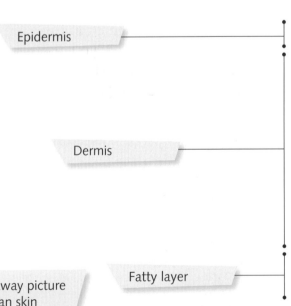

Epidermis

Dermis

Fatty layer

A cut–away picture of human skin

Where do we feel it?

Your whole body is covered with skin and you can feel with any part of your body. But, some parts can feel more than others. This is because some parts of the body have more nerve cells than other parts.

The picture shows what someone would look like if the size of their body parts matched the number of nerve cells they contained. You can see that hands are very sensitive. They have many nerve cells. Which parts of the hands are most sensitive?

Reflex action

We sometimes do things without even thinking because of our sense of touch and pain. If you stand on a thorn, you lift your foot quickly. The pain cells in your foot send a message to the spinal cord. This is a strong bundle of nerves in your backbone. The spinal cord sends the message on to the brain and causes you to react and lift your foot before you have time to think about it. This quick action is called a reflex action.

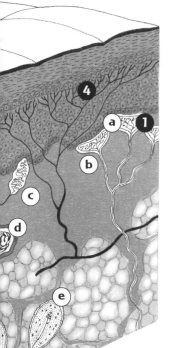

Key

1 Nerve cells
2 Hair follicle
3 Hair
4 Blood vessels
5 Sweat gland

Nerves which sense:
a Pain
b Heat
c Touch
d Cold
e Pressure

Blind people learn to read by touch using a system called Braille. The letters in Braille are made from raised dots which can be felt with the fingertips.

Some blind people can read about 100 words a minute by moving their fingertips across a page. How many words can you read in a minute using your eyes?

This is how you would write 'hello' in Braille.

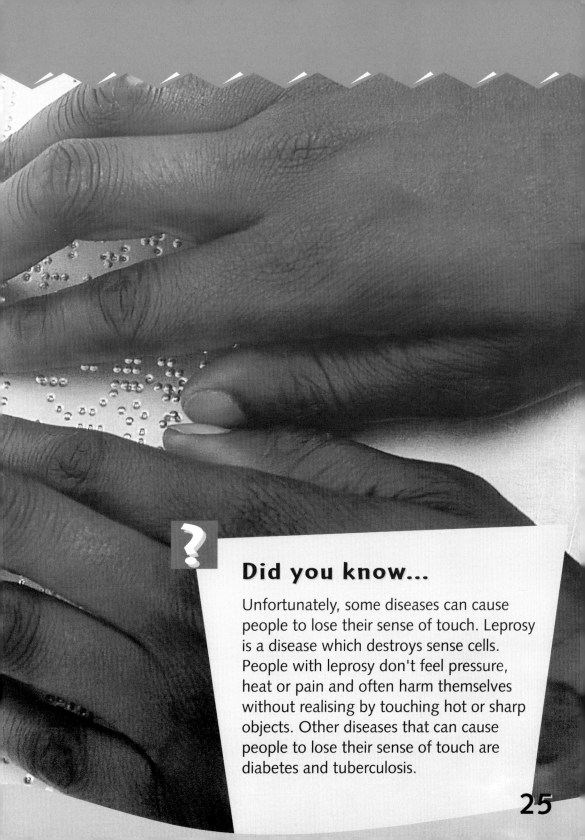

Did you know...

Unfortunately, some diseases can cause people to lose their sense of touch. Leprosy is a disease which destroys sense cells. People with leprosy don't feel pressure, heat or pain and often harm themselves without realising by touching hot or sharp objects. Other diseases that can cause people to lose their sense of touch are diabetes and tuberculosis.

Animals see

Animals that kill other animals, such as cheetah, normally have eyes at the front of their heads. This allows them to see their prey clearly when they are hunting. Animals that are hunted, such as buck and smaller mammals, usually have eyes on the sides of their heads. This helps them to see in all directions and to look out for their enemies.

It's amazing...

People can see all the colours of the rainbow and about ten million colour shades made from mixing the colours. But most birds can see even more colours than people! Honeybees can hardly see red, but they can see ultraviolet (UV) light on the leaves of flowers which guides them to the sugary nectar. People are totally blind to ultraviolet light.

Animals smell better than we do!

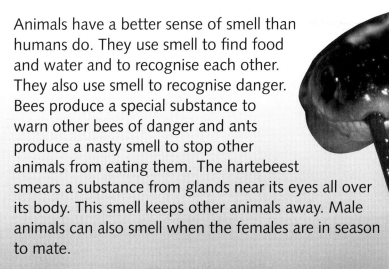

Animals have a better sense of smell than humans do. They use smell to find food and water and to recognise each other. They also use smell to recognise danger. Bees produce a special substance to warn other bees of danger and ants produce a nasty smell to stop other animals from eating them. The hartebeest smears a substance from glands near its eyes all over its body. This smell keeps other animals away. Male animals can also smell when the females are in season to mate.

Snakes have a special skin-like membrane at the back of their mouths called a Jacobson's organ. They use this organ to smell things. The tongue flicks out and is pulled back in over Jacobson's organ, which identifies the smell.

Can you taste with your feet?

Yes, if you are a locust! Some insects have taste buds on their tongues but others, like the locust, have them on their feet.

Fish have taste buds in their mouths and on the outside of their bodies. The taste buds on the body pick up the taste of particles in the water and send messages to the fish's brain. The brain tells the fish whether it is the taste of food or the taste of an enemy.

Animals can hear better than people

Most animals can hear better than we can. They can also make and hear sounds that we cannot hear. The table below shows the sounds that different animals can hear, from very high to very low frequencies.

How much do creatures hear?

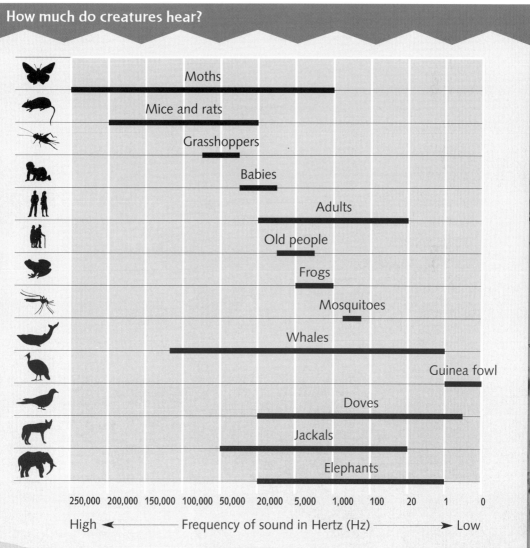

| | Moths |
| Mice and rats |
| Grasshoppers |
| Babies |
| Adults |
| Old people |
| Frogs |
| Mosquitoes |
| Whales |
| Guinea fowl |
| Doves |
| Jackals |
| Elephants |

250,000 200,000 150,000 100,000 50,000 20,000 5,000 1,000 100 20 1 0

High ◀— Frequency of sound in Hertz (Hz) —▶ Low

Snakes can sense other animals from a distance by feeling their vibrations on the ground. The snake feels these vibrations through the skin on its underbelly.

Fish can feel their prey and enemies in the water. They use the lateral line on the sides of their bodies to sense movements in the water.

Even some plants have a sense of touch!

Some leaves and flowers close up when they are touched. There are some carnivorous (meat-eating) species of plants that eat spiders, insects and even small animals. This Venus fly-trap knows when the insect has landed through sensors on its leaves. The leaves snap shut in about half a second and trap the insect inside.

The pictures show a Venus fly-trap waiting with open leaves. An insect lands inside shaking the leaf. The leaf snaps shut, trapping the insect inside.

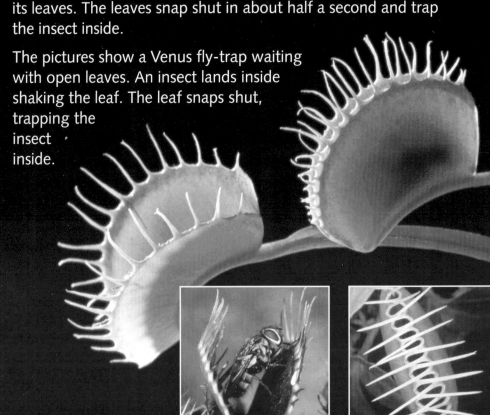

Glossary

cochlea the coiled spiral tube in the inner ear that receives sound waves and sends messages to the brain

decibel the unit of measurement for loudness

dermis the thicker inner layer of the skin

diabetes a disorder of the body in which too much sugar passes out of the body and not enough is stored

epidermis the outer layer of the skin

focus to direct an image clearly onto a surface, for example, the lens of the eye directs a clear image onto the retina

gland a cell or organ that produces a useful substance

image likeness or picture

imagine to think about something in your mind

interpret to make clear what something means

lateral line a line of sense cells on the sides of the body of a fish used to detect vibrations in the water

magnified made to appear much larger, for example, by using a lens or magnifying glass

mucus a wet slimy substance made by cells in the nose and lungs

nerve a fibre that carries messages from the sense organs to the brain and from the brain to the muscles

sensation a feeling of being aware of something

sound waves vibrations moving through the air

three-dimensional image an image you see that has depth rather than flatness

tuberculosis a disease of the lungs that can be passed from person to person

ultraviolet (UV) light invisible wavelengths of light from the sun

vapour tiny invisible droplets of water or another liquid in the air

vibrations movements to and fro

vitamins substances needed in the body in tiny amounts for good health

Index